Serge Mbele Amoungui

Python programming

Serge Mbele Amoungui

Python programming

Better PHP development with the Laravel Framework and Eloquent

ScienciaScripts

Imprint
Any brand names and product names mentioned in this book are subject to trademark, brand or patent protection and are trademarks or registered trademarks of their respective holders. The use of brand names, product names, common names, trade names, product descriptions etc. even without a particular marking in this work is in no way to be construed to mean that such names may be regarded as unrestricted in respect of trademark and brand protection legislation and could thus be used by anyone.

Cover image: www.ingimage.com

This book is a translation from the original published under ISBN 978-620-3-45593-9.

Publisher:
Sciencia Scripts
is a trademark of
Dodo Books Indian Ocean Ltd. and OmniScriptum S.R.L publishing group

120 High Road, East Finchley, London, N2 9ED, United Kingdom
Str. Armeneasca 28/1, office 1, Chisinau MD-2012, Republic of Moldova, Europe
Printed at: see last page
ISBN: 978-620-6-60441-9

Contents

Foreword

The Python language was ёle crёё in 1989 by Guido Van Rossum with the aim of creating a scripting language inspired by the ABC language, to be used as a command interpreter for the Amoeba operating system.

Over the following year, the language began to be adopted by the Amoeba project team, with Guido continuing its development mainly in his spare time. In February 1991, the first public version, numёrotёe 0.9.0, was posted on the Usenet forum. But this language continued to evolve after that date through the various compilers that came into being. Its international success has contributed to its adoption in the scientific community in particular.

This book has been designed as a Python programming course, although we are focusing on one of the most popular and widely used libraries in the scientific community, and more specifically the mathematical community, namely Numpy. While following a pedagogical approach, inherited from our teaching experience, we will always present the fundamental notions on one or more examples before giving more formally the gёnёral scope. The examples mentioned throughout the chapters allow for self-experimentation.

We have paid particular attention to the clarity and progressiveness of the presentation. The most technical points are only explained once the basics of the language are well established.

General information about paintings

Numpy

In this chapter, we provide an introduction to the concept of arrays in the Python language, using the Numpy library. Numpy is one of the most important basic libraries in the Python language, specialising in scientific computing in Python. Many Python libraries have built their foundation on the Numpy API, such as the Pandas library and Scipy. The same is true of more recent libraries such as scikit-learn and Tensorflow, which use Numpy arrays. The array is Numpy's main object; it is a grid-like structure containing data. An array can have any number of dimensions and each dimension can have any length. But the special thing about Numpy arrays is that all the elements are of the same type. In other words, a Numpy array cannot contain strings of characters, integers or floats...etc.

For the rest of this course, we will assume that you have the basics of the Python language.

1. Importing Numpy and creating tables

1.1. Importing from the Numpy library

To import the Numpy library into Python, we use the import instruction followed by the name of the library

import numpy as np

The **as np** syntax is a way of defining an alias so that it can be easily used in the code.

1.2. Creating tables

- **. Creating a one-dimensional array from a list**

First we create our Python list, then we invoke the **array** method to create an array of type ndarray of the Numpy object via its alias **np**

my_list = [3, 1, 5, 7, 10, 9, 6, 1, 8] array = np.array(my_list) print(type(array))

<class 'numpy.ndarray'>

- **. Creating a two-dimensional array from a list**

To create an n-dimensional Numpy array, we need to pass the list to the **np.array** method as follows:

my_list_of_lists = [

[6, 3, 5],

[5, 7, 2], [2, 3, 0]] np.array(my_list_of_lists)

```
array([[6,   3,     5],
[5, 7, 2],
[2, 3, 0]])
```

But if Python lists can include many different types of data, why do we still need arrays rather than lists? Firstly, Numpy arrays are more efficient in terms of execution speed, and secondly, element operations are not possible with Python lists. By default, lists are unidirectional and therefore do not allow vector or matrix operations. As a result, all the elements in a Numpy array must be of the same data type as each element in an array, since they must all be identical.

We can also create arrays from scratch using functions such as :

np.zeros()

np.random.random() np.arange()

- Creation of an array **np.zeros()**

The **np.zeros()** function is used to create an array filled with zeros. This numpy function takes as parameters a tuple indicating the number of rows and the number of columns.

np.zeros((5, 3))

array([[0., 0., 0.],

[0., 0., 0.],

[0., 0., 0.],

[0., 0., 0.],

[0., 0., 0.]])

- Creating an array with **np.random.random()**

The **np.random.random()** function is used to create an array of random numbers. This function also accepts a tuple defining the shape of the desired array, in other words the number of rows and the number of columns.

np.random.random((2, 4))

array([[0.15223805, 0.77584814, 0.59648901, 0.9859068], [0.82878832, 0.4931641,0.87801282,

0.32260836]])

- Creating an array with **np.arrange()**

The **np.arange** function is used to generate an interval of consecutive numbers. It creates an array of regularly-spaced numbers based on start and end values `np.arange(-1, 4)`

`array([-1, 0, 1, 2, 3])`

or np.arange(-1, 4, 2) with 2 taken to be the step.

`array([-1, 1, 3])`

1.3. The size of tables

In this section, we will discuss Numpy's ability to handle data of any dimension.

Just as we can create a two-dimensional array by feeding Numpy with a list of lists, we can create a 3D array by creating a list of lists (3D arrays).

`array1_2D = np.array([[1, 2],[3, 4]])`

`array2_2D = np.array([[8, 5],[6, 4]])`

`array3_2D = np.array([[8, 5],[6, 4]])`

`array_3D = np.array(array1_2D, array2_2D, array3_2D)`

In the jargon of Python programmers, a 2D array is called a matrix and an array with 3D or more is called a tensor. Numpy arrays embed a number of methods, such as the :

- .shape(): displays the dimension of an array `array_3D.shape`

`(3, 2, 2)`

- .flatten(): transforms a multi-dimensional array into a one-dimensional array

`array([1, 2, 3, 4, 8, 5, 6, 4, 8, 5, 6, 4])`

- .reshape(): this method resamples an array from one dimension to another, the function takes a tuple containing a number of rows and a number of columns.

-

```
my_array = np.array([[1,2], [5, 7], [5, 6]]) my_array.reshape((2, 3))

array([[1, 2, 5], [7, 5, 6]])
```

2. Types of Numpy donation

2.1. Numpy data types

The data type in NumPy is different from the primitive data types in Python, so Numpy data is more specific than Python data types in that Numpy data types include both integer and string data types. And the amount of memory available in bits is: np.int64, np.int32, np.float64, np.float32.

2.2. The dtype attribute

To find out the data type of a Numpy array, use the **".dtype"** attribute of the array object.

```
np.array([0.23, 4.47, 187.55]).dtype

dtype('float64')

np.array([[1,2,3,4],[5, 6, 7, 8]]).dtype

dtype('int32')

np.array(['Numpy', 'Course']).dtype

dtype('<U6')
```

2.3. Use dtype as argument

A data type can be declared when creating a Numpy array, using the optional keyword argument "dtype".

```
float_array = np.array([0.23, 4.47, 187.55], dtype=np.float32) float_array.dtype

dtype('float32')
```

2.4. Type conversion

To convert a numpy array into another type, use the ".astype" method in the array object, passing the type in question as a parameter.

boolean_array = np.array([[True, False], [False, False], [True, False]], dtype=np.bool_)

boolean_array.astype(np.int32)

array([[1, 0],

[0, 0],

[1, 0]])

Chapter 2

Data processing with Numpy

1. Indexing and splitting a table

We already know how to create arrays with Numpy, now we just need to know how to access, browse and sort the data. Like lists in Python, array indexing uses square brackets, and just as in Python the first index starts at zero, in Numpy the index also starts at zero.

- 2D element indexing

Indexing a two-dimensional array means giving it a row index and a column index in order to return a single element which is the join between the intersection of the row and the column. Consider the following two-dimensional array:

array_2D = np.array([[8, 5, 2, 4],[6, 4, 1, 0] ,[2, 4, 1, 6]]) array_2D

We want to access the first element of the second column array_2D[0, 1].

5

But if we give a numpy array a single index during indexing, this assumes that the index is a row index

array_2D[0]

array([8, 5, 2, 4])

- Splitting a table into 1D

To split the elements of an array, use the ":" symbol, defining the start and end positions on either side of the two points.

Syntax: array[start position : end position]

For example:

my_array = np.array([2, 4, 6, 8, 10])

my_array

my_array[2: 4]

array([6, 8])

- 2D table decoupage

For 2-dimensional slicing, numpy must be given information about how the rows and columns are to be sliced.

Syntax :

array[row start position: row end position, column start position: column end position]

example: array_2D[0:2, 1:3]

array([[5, 2], [4, 1]])

2. Filtering elements in an array

There are two main ways of filtering data in a table in numpy, and each is useful in different situations. To do this, you need two things to filter the data in an array

- Creating a mask with indexing

- Use the np.where(...) function

a. Creating a Boolean mask

The code for creating a mask checks whether a condition is true for each element in an array

```
array_of_five = np.arange(1, 6)
array_of_five
array([1, 2, 3, 4, 5])
```

To filter the array so that it only includes odd numbers, we first create a "boolean mask".

```
mask = array_of_five%2 != 0
mask
array([ True, False, True, False, True])
```

Once we've created our "mask boolean" indicating for which elements the condition is true, we can index the array using the mask.

```
array_of_five[mask]
array([1, 3, 5])
```

The mask should be considered as providing the indices of all the elements where the condition is true. In the case of numbers from 1 to 5, only 1, 3 and 5 are not divisible by two.

We may want to filter according to a condition in one row or column, but return data from another.

This is the table below:

```
key_and_value = np.array([[2, 12], [2, 21], [4, 33], [5, 27]]) key_and_value array([[ 2, 12], [ 2, 21], [ 4, 33], [ 5, 27]])
```

Suppose we assign key/value pairs in an array and we want to know which keys in the array have an even number of values. The array keys are in the left-hand column and the array values are in the right-hand column.

First, let's create a mask that checks which values in the second column are divisible by two.

```
key_and_value[:, 0]%2 == 0
```

Next, let's index the first column using this mask so that we return the key for the rows where the size of the class in the first column meets the condition.

```
key_and_value[:, 1][key_and_value[:, 0]%2 == 0]
array([12, 21, 33])
```

b. Using np.where

Applying the np.where() method in the previous example returns indices indicating that the array with indices zeros, one and two have an even number of elements.

np.where(key_and_value[:, 0]%2 == 0) (array([0, 1, 2], dtype=int64),)

Note that the index array is enclosed in brackets; in reality, the np.where() function returns a tuple of arrays. But why return a tuple of arrays? Quite simply because when we're dealing with a multi-dimensional filter array, each element can only be located by including an index for each dimension.

Let's use np.where() to return the indices of zero in our array dataset.

Consider the initial dimension table 3 in Chapter I :

my_array = np.array([

[0, 0, 4, 3, 0, 0, 2, 0, 9],

[0, 4, 2, 9, 1, 0, 2, 0, 0],

[0, 3, 2, 8, 1, 0, 7, 0, 0],

[0, 6, 2, 5, 1, 0, 2, 4, 0],

])

Now, np.where() returns two sets of indices one for row indices and one for column indices, since identifying each individual zero requires both a row and column index.

row_ind, column_ind = np.where(my_array == 0) row_ind, column_ind (array([0, 0, 0, 0, 0, 1, 1, 1, 1, 2, 2, 2, 2, 3, 3, 3], dtype=int64),

array([0, 1, 4, 5, 7, 0, 5, 7, 8, 0, 5, 7, 8, 0, 5, 8], dtype=int64))

it is very important to decompress the results of **np.where()** into different variables.

c. Search and replace

The feature that makes np.where() really powerful is its ability to check whether rows, columns or elements meet a given condition.

```
np.where(my_array==0,'', my_array) array([[-1, -1,    4,    3,   -1,   -1,    2,
     -1,    9],
 [-1,   4,    2,    9,    1,   -1,    2,   -1,   -1],
 [-1,   3,    2,    8,    1,   -1,    7,   -1,   -1],
 [-1,   6,    2,    5,    1,   -1,    2,    4,   -1]]])
```

For example, to replace all the zeros in the previous **my_array** with -1s, we need to pass the number -1 as the second argument to np.where, the third argument being the alternative in case the condition is not met. Here, we want the non-zero elements to remain unchanged, so we pass the original array to signify this.

d. Adding and deleting data

In this section we'll look at how to add and remove elements in a Numpy array, which is an important skill in data processing because the data isn't always as you'd expect or as it should be.

- Concatenation in numpy

17	11	3
6	8	7
12	15	13

+

7	1
32	8
3	11

=

17	11	3	7	1
6	8	7	32	8
12	15	13	3	11

Concatenation in numpy refers to adding data to an array along any axis, like adding columns to a 2-dimensional array. To do this, concatenation is performed using the :np.concatenate() function.

- Concatenation of lines

Let's go back to our key/value table and add information from two other key/value pairs. We now have:

array_key_value = np.array([[2, 11], [2, 21], [3, 26], [4, 25]]) new_array = np.array([[5, 30],

[5, 17]])

To concatenate the two arrays, pass a tuple of array names to the np.concatenate() function.

np.concatenate((array_key_value, new_array))

array([[2, 11],

[2, 21],

[3, 26],

[4, 25],

[5, 30],

[5, 17]])

In our case, we are adding new lines, in other words we are concatenating along the first axis. As concatenation along the first axis is the default value, the behaviour of np.concatenate() means that we don't need to explicitly indicate which axis to concatenate along. To concatenate along other dimensions, you need to define the axis keyword as an argument.

- Compatibility of table shapes and sizes

It is important that the tables to be concatenated have compatible shapes, in other words, they must have the same number of columns. More specifically, they must have the same shape along all axes, except the one being concatenated. For example, concatenating an array (3x3) with an array (4,2) gives a ValueError.

<table>
<tr><td>12</td><td>11</td><td>3</td></tr>
<tr><td>7</td><td>8</td><td>6</td></tr>
<tr><td>11</td><td>15</td><td>13</td></tr>
</table>

\+

<table>
<tr><td>7</td><td>2</td></tr>
<tr><td>33</td><td>18</td></tr>
<tr><td>3</td><td>11</td></tr>
<tr><td>15</td><td>5</td></tr>
</table>

=

ValueError: all the input array dimension for the concatenation axis must match exactly

Whatever axis (horizontal, vertical) we concatenate on, because no part of this form is compatible, vertically we have 4 rows compared to 3 rows and horizontally two columns compared to 3 columns. So ValueError reminds us that the dimensions of the array for the concatenation axis must match exactly. We can concatenate an array (3x3) with an array (3x2), because the axis we are concatenating along, the second axis, is the only axis that does not have the same length.

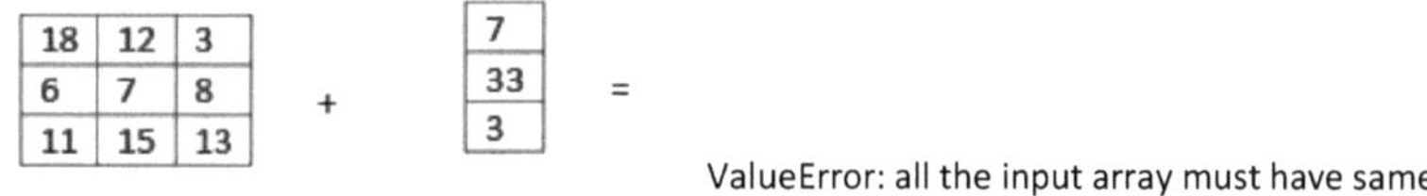

- Dimensional compatibility

ValueError: all the input array must have same number of dimension

For a successful concatenation of two arrays, the two arrays must also have the same number of dimensions. This is particularly important to remember when concatenating a single row or column of data, usually kept in a 1D array, with a 2D array.

So, to solve the above problem, you need to add a single row or column, turn the 1D table into a 2D table using the **".reshape"** method **(see Chapter I)** before adding the column.

- Creating compatibility

To reshape a 1D array for concatenation with a 2D array, indicate whether the data is vertical or horizontal by defining a value of 1 as the length of the flat dimension.

Array_1D = array([1,2 ,3])

Column_array_2D = Array_1D.reshape((3,1))

Column_array_2D

array([[1],

[2], [3]])

A table containing a single column, like this one, will have a length of 1 along the second axis. An array containing a single row will have a length of 1 along the first axis.

row_array_2D = array_1D.reshape((1, 3))

row_array_2D

array([[1, 2, 3]])

NB: It is impossible to add new dimensions with np.concatenate, as the function only adds data along an existing axis. Adding new dimensions is possible by using other functions which we will discuss later in the course.

e. Deleting data with np.delete

We can delete elements in a numpy array with the function np.delete(...),

which takes three arguments

- The table to be deleted

- An index or array of indexes to delete

- The axis to be removed

data = np.array([[1, 22, 1, 5], [2, 21, 1, 4], [3, 28, 3, 7], [4, 25, 3, 4]]) data

array([[1, 22, 1, 5],

[2, 21, 1, 4],

[3, 28, 3, 7],

[4, 25, 3, 4]])

If np.delete(data, 1, axis=0), we get array([[1, 22, 1, 5], [3, 28, 3, 7], [4, 25, 3, 4]])

For example, to delete the second row of a 2D array, the index to delete

will be 1, and the deletion will occur along the first axis, represented by a

zero.

To delete the second column instead, update the axis argument to 1

(axis=1)

We have: np.delete(data, 1, axis=1) array ([[1, 1, 5], [2, 1, 4], [3, 3, 7], [4, 3, 4]])

Chapter 3

Summarising data with Numpy

1 Data summary

It's very common to ask general questions about what's in the data when we first look at a data set. Numpy has several excellent ways of summarising the information in a table. We will review the following aggregation methods:

- Sum()

- Min()

- Max()

- Mean()

- Cumsum()

a. Application of aggregation methods

Let's imagine we're a security company with four major clients. We have a count of intrusions by detection alarms on our customers' premises.

alarm_security = np.array([[1 3 0 1]

[0, 1, 2, 0],

[1, 1, 0, 3],

[2, 1, 2, 1], [0, 0, 0, 0]

])

alarm_security

	Custome Client1	Custome r2	Custome r3	r4
Year1	1	3	0	1
Year2	0	1	2	0
Year3	1	1	0	3
Year4	2	1	2	1
Year5	0	0	0	0

array([[1, 3, 0, 1],

[0, 1, 2, 0],

[1, 1, 0, 3],

[2, 1, 2, 1],

[0, 0, 0, 0]])

Each row of data here represents the number of intruder alarm signals that occurred in a given year, and each column represents the alarm signal for each customer. To better understand our data, it's important to look at some summary values.

Our first aggregation method is .sum(), which adds up all the elements in the numpy array. We can see that over the five years we've been recording intruder alarm signals, we've identified a total of 19 intrusions.

So: np.sum(alarm_security) = 19

We can control the axis to be added with the **"axis"** argument

alarm_security.sum(axis=0)

	Client1	Client2	Client3	Client4
Year1	1	3	0	1
Year2	0	1	2	0
Year3	1	1	0	3
Year4	2	1	2	1
Year5	0	0	0	0
	Σ	Σ	Σ	Σ

array([4, 6, 4, 5])

By setting the **axis** argument equal to zero, we add up the values of all the rows in each column, creating column totals. In this case, each total represents the number of security alarma breaches a customer has already experienced. Customer two has had many breaches.

Defining the axis equal to 1 will add the values of all the columns in each row, creating row totals.

	Client1	Client2	Client3	Client4	
Year1	1	3	0	1	Σ
Year2	0	1	2	0	Σ
Year3	1	1	0	3	Σ
Year4	2	1	2	1	Σ
Year5	0	0	0	0	Σ

alarm_security.sum(axis=1)

array([5, 3, 5, 6, 0])

Here the totals represent the security red flags experienced by customers over the course of each year.

NB: It can be confusing at first to know whether the axis argument should refer to columns or rows.

If we want a column representing the sum of the elements across the rows, the end result is a single column, so the axis is set to 1.

Many aggregation methods use the same syntax as .sum(), i.e. calculating the minimum and maximum, e.g. :

```
alarm_security.min()                              alarm_security.max()

> 0                                               > 3
```

This allows us to find the minimum or maximum of an array of integers if no axis argument is defined. According to the example, the smallest number of violations suffered by a customer in a given year is 0 and the largest is 3. And we can find the minimum and maximum of each column or each row if the axis argument is set to 0 or 1.

```
alarm_security.min(axis=0)                        alarm_security.min(axis=1)
> array([0, 0, 0, 0])                             > array([0, 0, 0, 1, 0])
```

The average number of intrusion attacks a customer can expect over the course of a year is around 0.95.

```
alarm_security.mean()
> 0.95
```

If the axis is equal to 1, we obtain the average number of offences per year for all customers.

```
alarm_security.mean(axis=1)
> array([1.25, 0.75, 1.25, 1.5 , 0.  ])
```

For example, the average number of offences in the first year was 1.25.

b. The keepdims argument

The keepdims argument is an operational argument offered by the .sum(), .min(), .max(), .mean() methods. This argument is set to True if the dimensions which are reduced during aggregation are left in the output array and set to 1.

```
alarm_security.sum(axis=1, keepdims=True)

> array([[5],
[3],
[5],
[6], [0]] )
```

c. Cumulative sums

The np.cumsum() method is used to return the cumulative sum of elements along a given axis. For example, when the axis argument is set to zero, np.cumsum() returns the number of security waits a customer has had up to this year.

```
alarm_security.cumsum(axis=0) > array([[1,      3,    0,    1],
[1, 4, 2,    1],
[2, 5, 2,    4],
[4, 6, 4,    5],
[4, 6, 4,    5]])
```

d. Vectorisation operations

Vectorized operations are one of the most important concepts in Numpy. Remember the numpy rule introduced in Chapter I, according to which all the elements of an array must be of the same data type. It is thanks to this rule that Numpy is able to perform these tasks, under the bonnet Numpy externalizes these tasks to the C language, which is a low level programming language like assembler, known for its speed and efficient use of memory, and yes Numpy is a brick built around the C language. Using C code optimised in this way is known as **vectorisation**. This whole part of the course will be based on the use of vectorised operations.

For example, the sum method uses C under the bonnet to add up quickly and efficiently. Take the following example:

1	2	3
4	5	6

+ 3 =

4	5	6
7	8	9

One of the advantages of using vectorised operations is that it considerably reduces the amount of code we have to write, but also the time it takes to execute it. For example, using Python to add the number three to each element of an array requires us to write a for loop, which increases the level of complexity and execution time.

```
arr = np.array([[1, 2, 3],[4, 5, 6]])

for row in range(arr.shape[0]):

for column in range(arr.shape[1]):

arr[row][column]+=3

array([[4, 5, 6],

[7, 8, 9]])
```

As you can see, this is a lot of code for a simple task and for loops are slow by their very nature, as the loop has to be executed for each element one at a time. The syntax is more efficient and simple with Numpy. We use a plus sign and tell numpy what unique number we'd like to add to all the elements in the array. This unique number is often referred to as a scalar. We therefore add a scalar, i.e. 3, to each element in our array.

- Multiplication by a scalar

We can use a similar syntax to multiply an array by a scalar.

```
arr = np.array([[1, 2, 3], [4, 5, 6]]) arr*3
array([[ 3, 6, 9],
[12, 15, 18]])
```

- Adding two paintings together

Vectorised operations also allow us to perform addition, multiplication, subtraction and division operations between arrays of the same shape. When we add two arrays of the same shape together, Numpy will add each element in the first array to the element in the same location in the second array.

```
arr_1 = np.array([[1, 2, 3], [4, 5, 6]])
arr_2 = np.array([[1, 0, 0], [1, 0, 1]])
arr_1 + arr_2
array([[2, 2, 3],
[5, 5, 7]])
```

The principle is the same for multiplying two arrays together, as well as for subtracting, dividing, moduli ... etc. The operations are performed between the elements in the corresponding positions in each array.

NB: Although vector operations work extremely well with mathematics and numbers, they are exploited throughout Numpy. We used them to create Boolean masks and filter arrays in the last chapter.

Here's a boolean mask indicating where the elements in the array are greater than three, filtered using vectorised syntax.

```
arr = np.array([[1, 2, 3], [4, 5, 6]]) arr > 3
array([[False, False, False],
[ True, True, True]])
```

e. Crfeer our own vectorisation functions

We can even create our own vectorized functions from Python functions using np.vectorize()

```
arr = np.array(['This', 'is', 'awesome', 'library'])

len(arr) > 2

> True
```

We might expect the Numpy vectorised syntax to check whether the length of each element in the array is greater than two. In our case this doesn't work, instead the code returns **True**, because the array has more than two elements. The reason our code behaved the way it did is that **len** is a Python function, not a Numpy function, so it can't vectorise. For the **len** function to be able to vectorise, we need to feed it to the **np.vectorize()** function without putting the brackets around it, so we can convert it into a vectorised Numpy function, as follows:

```
vec_ = np.vectorize(len)
```

Then we pass the array as an argument and this gives us the result we were hoping for

```
vec_ = np.vectorize(len)

vec_(arr) > 2

array([ True, False, True])
```

f. Generalities about Broadcasting in Numpy

One of the vectorised operations we're talking about is diffusion. We have previously discussed vectorised operations between arrays of the same size or between an array and a scalar. It is also possible to perform mathematical operations between arrays of different shapes. For this purpose, broadcasting is the stretching of a smaller array over a larger one.

5	7	13
6	10	12
11	8	1

+

2
5
10

- Scattering a scalar

In fact, adding a scalar to an array uses broadcasting. Here, the scalar two (3) that we add to each element of the array **arr** is broadcast across the array so that the result is the same as if the array had been added to a full array of two.

5	7	13
6	10	12
11	8	1

+ 3 =

8	10	16
9	13	15
14	11	4

This operation is equivalent to the following

5	7	13
6	10	12
11	8	1

\+

3	3	3
3	3	3
3	3	3

\=

8	10	16
9	13	15
14	11	4

The difference is that broadcasting is more efficient in terms of memory and computing power.

- Compatibility rule

Broadcast only works with compatible displayboards

Shape(10, 5)

Shape(10, 1)

To determine whether the boards are broadcastable, compare the dimensions of the board from right to left. Each set of dimensions must be compatible for the boards to be diffusable.

A table with 10 rows and 5 columns can be distributed with a table with 10 rows and 1 column.

A 10x5 table can also be displayed with a 1D table with 5 elements, since the rightmost dimensions are both 5.

Two paintings do not need to have the same number of dimensions to be broadcast.

A 10x5 panel cannot be distributed with a 5x10 panel because no set of dimensions is compatible.

Finally, an array of dimensions (10x5) is not compatible with a 1D array of 10 elements, since the rightmost set of dimensions is not compatible.

Line broadcasting

0	1	2	3	4
5	6	7	8	9

+

0	1	2	3	4

=

0	2	4	6	8
5	7	9	11	13

```
arr = np.arange(10).reshape((2, 5))

arr + np.array([0, 1, 2, 3, 4])

array([[ 0, 2, 4, 6, 8], [ 5, 7, 9, 11, 13]])
```

Add a table containing numbers from zero to four to a 2D table. Content the numbers from zero to nine with two rows and five columns. These arrays are broadcastable because they all have a final dimension of five. Numpy broadcasts the 1D table by operating as if there were one copy of the 1D table for each row of the 2D table, then adding the two sets together.

0	1	2	3	4
5	6	7	8	9

+

0	1	2	3	4
0	1	2	3	4

=

0	2	4	6	8
5	7	9	11	13

- Incompatible Broadcasting

0	1	2	3	4
5	6	7	8	9

+

0	1

=

ValueError: operand could not be broadcast together with shape (2, 5) (2,)

```
array = np.arange(10).reshape((2, 5))

array + np.array([0, 1])
```

Numpy's default assumption is that the user tries to broadcast by row, as we saw in the previous example. For example, a 1D array of two elements cannot be broadcast on an array with two rows and 5 columns, because the rightmost dimension of each array is not the same.

Broadcasting columns

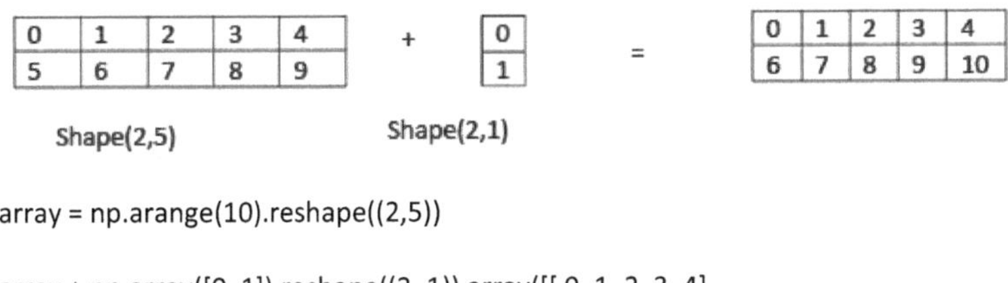

array = np.arange(10).reshape((2,5))

array + np.array([0, 1]).reshape((2, 1)) array([[0, 1, 2, 3, 4],

[6, 7, 8, 9, 10]])

We can spread an array of two elements over an array of two rows by modifying its shape using point reshaping so that the end dimensions are compatible. Now the array to be stretched has two rows and one column. Since an end dimension of one is compatible with any other back dimension, the arrays can be spread together. Again, the calculation is performed as if the single-column array had been stretched over an array of the same shape as the larger array.

The advantage of distribution increases with the size of the data we are working with.

1	2
3	4

X

5
10

=

5	10
30	30

1	2
3	4

−

5	10

=

-4	-8
-2	-6

The same logic applies to multiplication and subtraction.
Multiplying by a column multiplies the column by both columns in the larger table. Subtracting a row subtracts the row from both columns.

Chapter 4

Introduction to image processing

Since images are represented in array form, we can also use the Numpy library to perform various image processing tasks. In this chapter, we will learn about image processing tasks using Numpy. In general, we use Numpy to perform mathematical operations on data, which is usually represented in the form of arrays. Since images can also be considered as arrays, we can also use Numpy to perform various image processing tasks.

a. Loading an image

As we saw in the introductory chapter, it's important to install the Numpy library first of all, but we'll also need the Matplotlib library in order to load and display the rendered image processed via Numpy. So let's install the various libraries from your console or command prompt, or type **pip install numpy matplotlib** in the console. Then you need to import the libraries in order to manipulate them. To import the libraries type :

```
import numpy as np
import matplotlib.pyplot as plt %matplotlib inline
```

In order to process images, we first need to load the image. To do this, we use the imread() method, which takes the url of the image as a parameter.

```
image = plt.imread("C:/Users/guera/Images/book/comment4.jpg") print(image)
    [[[220 192 171]
    [220 192 171]
    [220 192 171]
    [217 188 170]
    [217 189 168]
    [217 189 168]]
```

```
[   [220192171]

    [220192171]

    [220192171]

    [218189171]

    [218189171]

    [218190169]]

[[222 194 173]

[222  194  173]

[222  194  173]

...

[219  190  172]

[219  190  172]

           170]

[219  191  ]

[[146 125 108]

[217  190  181]

[236  208  204]

...

[

    4

9    27  14]

[

    9

6    74  63]

[243  223 212] ]

[[150 128 114]

[212  185  174]

[240  211  205]

...

[178  156  142]

[135  113  100]

[243  224  210] ]
```

```
[[137 118  101]

[205  177  165]

[234  202  191]

...

[215  194  177]

[234  215  200]

[234  215  200]]]
```

So we can see the numerical form of an image, knowing that images are made up of pixel values in this output above, we can see that the image is essentially an array or a Numpy array in our case. Because of this, we can also plot it using the matplotlib library, to do this we use the imshow() method which takes the previous image variable as a parameter.

```
imgplot = plt.imshow(image)
```

The result is as follows:

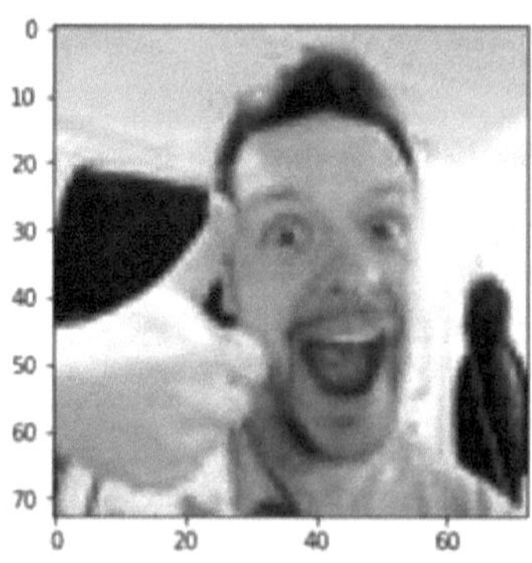

b. Display image details

It's important for us to know the size, shape and data type of an image. To check the size of 1 image, we use the image.size property

```python
print('image size: ',image.ndim)

print('image shape: ',image.shape)

print('the type: ',image.dtype)

print('pixel value a [R, G, B]', image[40, 40])

print('min pixel value in channel B', image[:, :, 2].min())
```

The result is as follows:

image size: 3

shape of an image: (73, 73, 3)

the type: uint8

pixel value a [R, G, B] [218 109 78]

min pixel value at channel B 0

NB: to save an image, you need to execute the instruction image.save(), passing it the path where to store the image and the name of the image as well as its extension, png, jpeg, etc.

c. Cropping an image

Once the image has been loaded, it's time to perform some operations on it. One of the most basic operations is the basic cropping of our image. With Numpy, one of the most basic ways of cropping an image is to cut out the table.

```python
_img = image[20:149,:150,:]
imgplot = plt.imshow(_img)
```

d. RGB channel display

Each image is made up of pixel values and these pixel values represent three integers known as the RGB value. To separate the image into these colours, we need to extract the correct slice from the image array.

```
fig, axs = plt.subplots(nrows=1, ncols=3, figsize=(22,10))

for f, ax in zip(range(3), axs):

_img = np.zeros(image.shape, dtype="uint8")

_img[:,:,f] = image[:,:,f] ax.imshow(_img)
```

We can see that we've separated the RGB of the image for this, we've mapped the values between 0 and 1 and converted them to type uint8.

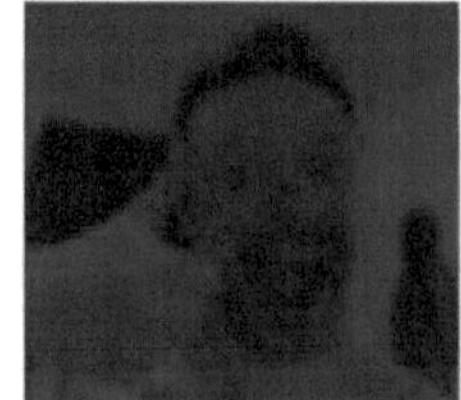

e. Reverse resolution

The resolution of an image can be inverted by subtracting the pixel value from the maximum value (255 for unit8).

```
import numpy as np

from PIL import Image

img = np.array(Image.open('C:/Users/guera/OneDrive/Images/book/comment4.jpg'))

_im = 255 - img
```

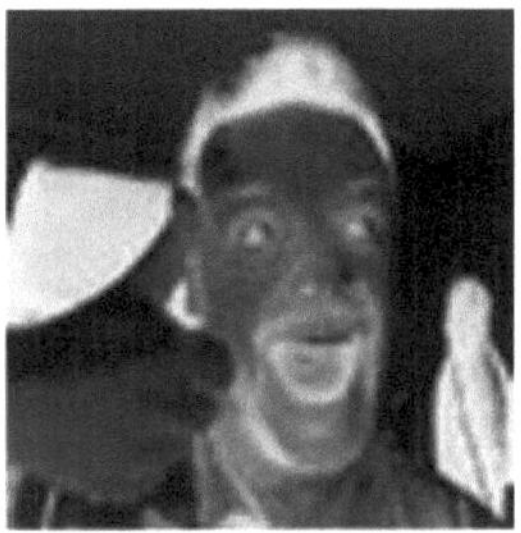

```
Image.fromarray(_im).save('C:/Users/guera/OneDrive/Images/book/inverse.jpg')
```

f. Reverse resolution

It is possible to reduce the colour density of an image by cutting off the remainder of the integer division and multiplying it again, so that the pixel values become discrete and the number of colours can be reduced.

```
import numpy as np

from PIL import Image

im = np.array(Image.open('C:/Users/guera/Images/book/comment4.jpg'))

img = {str(i): im//i*i for i in [32, 64, 128]}

_im = np.concatenate((im, img['32'], img['64'], img['128']), axis=1)

Image.fromarray(_im).save('C:/Users/guera/Images/book/comment6.png')
```

References and useful links

https://betterprogramming.pub/numpy-illustrated-the-visual-guide-to-numpy-3b1d4976de1d

https://github.com/numpy/numpy-tutorials

https://github.com/rougier/numpy-100

https://dl-nlp.github.io/numpy_intro.pdf

https://www.math.univ-toulouse.fr/~cbesse/mesassets/teaching/SpocPython/Files/V_Libraries/i_learn.pdf

http://web.mit.edu/dvp/Public/numpybook.pdf

https://www.labri.fr/perso/nrougier/from-python-to-numpy/

Printed by Books on Demand GmbH, Norderstedt / Germany